D1084881

GREAT SMOKY MOUNTAINS

NATIONAL PARK

by Maddie Spalding

Content Consultant
Daniel Pierce, PhD
Department of History
University of North Carolina at Asheville

Core Library

An Imprint of Abdo Publishing
abdopublishing.com

abdopublishing.com

Published by Abdo Publishing, a division of ABDO, PO Box 398166, Minneapolis, Minnesota 55439. Copyright © 2017 by Abdo Consulting Group, Inc. International copyrights reserved in all countries. No part of this book may be reproduced in any form without written permission from the publisher. Core Library™ is a trademark and logo of Abdo Publishing.

Printed in the United States of America, North Mankato, Minnesota
082016
012017

Cover Photo: Dean Fikar/iStockphoto
Interior Photos: Dean Fikar/iStockphoto, 1; Jo Crebbin/Shutterstock Images, 4; Superstock/Everett Collection, 9; Anton Foltin/Shutterstock Images, 10; Nickolay Khoroshkov/Shutterstock Images, 12; Thomas Takacs/iStockphoto, 15; Red Line Editorial, 17; Dean Fikar/Shutterstock Images, 18; Adrian Ciurea/Shutterstock Images, 23; Lindsey Heffernan/PA Game Commission, 24; NativeStock/North Wind Picture Archives, 26; Nancy Carter/North Wind Picture Archives, 29; Stania Kasula/Alamy, 32; Jon Bilous/Shutterstock Images, 34, 45; Joel Carillet/iStockphoto, 37; Shutterstock Images, 39; Jeffrey M. Frank/Shutterstock Images, 40; National Park Service, 42–43

Editor: Mirella Miller
Series Designer: Ryan Gale

Publisher's Cataloging-in-Publication Data

Names: Spalding, Maddie, author.
Title: Great Smoky Mountains National Park / by Maddie Spalding.
Description: Minneapolis, MN : Abdo Publishing, 2017. | Series: National parks
    | Includes bibliographical references and index.
Identifiers: LCCN 2016945463 | ISBN 9781680784749 (lib. bdg.) |
    ISBN 9781680798593 (ebook)
Subjects: LCSH: Great Smoky Mountains National Park (N.C. and Tenn.)--
    Juvenile literature.
Classification: DDC 976.8/89--dc23
LC record available at http://lccn.loc.gov/2016945463

CONTENTS

CHAPTER ONE

LAND OF THE BLUE SMOKE

It is evening in Great Smoky Mountains National Park. The sky has turned a pale pink. Trees blanket the mountains. Fog settles along the treetops. A sea of gold, red, and green autumn leaves slopes down the mountainside. A male elk paws at the ground in the Cataloochee Valley below. His breath steams in the cool air. He approaches a female elk. He tilts back his antlered head. A high-pitched screech

An elk's bugle call echoes through the mountainside of the Smokies.

Protecting Wildlife

A male elk's bugle call signals the start of fall in Great Smoky Mountains National Park. But it signifies more than the changing season. It also reminds visitors of the park's commitment to protecting wildlife. Overhunting and habitat loss eliminated the region's elk population in the mid-1800s. But the National Park Service was committed to bringing them back. It began reintroducing elk into the area in 2001. Now these animals thrive, along with more than 400 other animal species.

issues from his throat. It warns other male elk to stay far away.

Scenic Views

More than 10 million people visit Great Smoky Mountains National Park each year. This makes it the most popular US national park. It stretches across the border between North Carolina and Tennessee. Its 522,427 acres (211,419 ha) of land are divided almost evenly between these two states. The western section of the Appalachian Mountains crosses through the park. This segment of mountains is called the Great Smoky Mountains, or the Smokies. These peaks are some of the tallest in the Appalachian Mountains chain.

Fog often hugs the peaks of the Smokies. This fog looks similar to wisps of smoke. Trees produce hydrocarbons. Hydrocarbons mix with moisture in the air. This creates a blue fog. Cherokee Indians who once lived in the area called the mountains "Shaconage." This means "Land of the Blue Smoke."

PERSPECTIVES
Park Ranger Bob Miller

Bob Miller has been a park ranger for more than 20 years. He describes the strangest thing he has ever seen:

We had a bear turned loose. . . . This bear . . . acted just like a big dog: licking people's hands, rubbing against their legs, and just plain begging. We couldn't take a chance on leaving him up there for fear he'd either injure somebody or would himself be a victim of aggression by another bear. . . . So after umpteen phone calls we were able to find an accredited wildlife park in Ohio that would accept him.

Early Conservationists

Approximately 80 percent of Great Smoky Mountains National Park is covered in forests. This was not the case in the early 1900s. Logging companies were clearing trees at a rapid rate. More than 300,000 acres (121,400 ha) of forest had been cut by the mid-1920s.

Nature writer Horace Kephart was shocked by this transformation. Kephart had lived in the Smokies since 1904. The land had been unspoiled then. But the booming timber business was quickly damaging the environment.

Kephart wrote articles about the Smokies for newspapers. He became friends with photographer George Masa. Masa was also concerned about the future of the Smokies. Kephart and Masa teamed up to create a booklet for the Great Smoky Mountains Conservation Association (GSMCA) in 1925. The GSMCA was a group of community leaders from nearby towns.

The GSMCA hoped its photographs and writing would convince the government to create a national park for visitors.

Funding the Park

The US Congress authorized the creation of the park in 1926. But Tennessee and North Carolina had to come up with $10 million to fund it. Donations reached $5 million in 1927. Conservationist John D. Rockefeller Jr. donated another $5 million in 1928. But the government could not begin development. Thousands of white and Cherokee settlers still lived

Great Smoky Mountains National Park was expanded into the park visitors see today.

on the land. Some sold their land willingly. Others fought to keep their land.

By 1934 Tennessee and North Carolina had purchased 300,000 acres (121,400 ha) of land in the Smokies. Smokies settlers who had signed leases that gave them lifetime ownership of their land were allowed to stay temporarily. But they were not allowed to cut down trees or hunt. The land was protected as Great Smoky Mountains National Park.

Though Great Smoky Mountains National Park was established in 1934, its dedication ceremony did not happen until 1940. Here, President Franklin D. Roosevelt declared his support:

> *In this Park, we shall conserve these trees. . . . We used up or destroyed much of our natural heritage just because that heritage was so bountiful. We slashed our forests, we used our soils . . . all of this so greatly that we were brought rather suddenly to face the fact that unless we gave thought to the lives of our children and grandchildren, they would no longer be able to live and to improve upon our American way of life. In these later years we have tried sincerely and honestly to look ahead to the future years. We are at last definitely engaged in the task of conserving the bounties of nature.*

> Source: "Franklin D. Roosevelt: Address at Dedication of Great Smoky Mountains National Park." The American Presidency Project. The University of California, Santa Barbara, n.d. Web. Accessed April 22, 2016.

Consider Your Audience

Review this passage closely. Consider how you would adapt it for a different audience, such as your teacher or your friends. Write a blog post conveying this same information for the new audience. What is the most effective way to get your point across to this audience? How does your new approach differ from the original text and why?

CHAPTER TWO

GEOLOGICAL HISTORY

The peaks that make up the Smokies run in an unbroken chain for more than 36 miles (58 km). Elevation ranges from 876 to 6,643 feet (267 to 2,025 m).

Earth is made up of tectonic plates. These are large segments of land. They move slowly and sometimes collide. The force of these collisions can push up rocks along faults. Faults are fractures

The Smokies are among the oldest mountain ranges in the world.

in Earth's surface. This buildup of rocks can form mountains. The Smokies were formed this way.

The North American plate collided with the African plate between 310 and 245 million years ago. The force from the collision lifted up rocks. Older rocks were pushed on top of younger rocks along a fault geologists call the Great Smoky Fault. This process continued for millions of years. The uplifted rocks gradually formed the Smokies and the entire Appalachian mountain chain.

Approximately 200 million years ago, the North American and African plates separated. But the mountains remained. The Smokies were much taller

The tower at Clingmans Dome has great views of the park since it is the tallest peak at 6,643 feet (2,025 m).

than they are now. Some geologists estimate they were more than 27,000 feet (8,230 m) tall. But wind, rain, ice, and snow began to erode the mountain rock.

Ancient Rocks

The Smokies are made up of layers of rocks. The youngest rocks form the base of the mountains. These are cemented sand, silt, and clay. They date from between 450 and 545 million years ago.

Older rocks form the top and middle layers of mountain peaks. Many are between 800 and

Junior Ranger Program

First Lady Michelle Obama launched the Let's Move Outside Junior Ranger Program in 2010. It encourages children to exercise in outdoor environments. At Great Smoky Mountains National Park, they can explore and learn about the park while getting exercise. National Park Service Director Jon Jarvis praises this program. He says: "Young people inspire us; we want to help them be vigorous and curious for life. It starts with family fun. National parks are amazing places where exercise is disguised as adventure, and we sneak in some learning too."

545 million years old. Some are more than 1 billion years old. Heat and pressure during mountain formation hardened these rocks.

Igneous rocks are noticeable because of their dark color. These rocks were formed from volcanic lava. Lava spouted from volcanoes. As it cooled, it formed igneous rocks. There are no volcanoes in or near Great Smoky National Park today. But igneous rocks hint at the area's volcanic past.

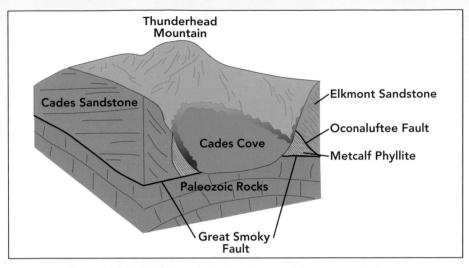

Varied Elevations

The Smokies are made up of layers of rocks. This image shows the layers of rocks that surround Cades Cove, a valley on the west side of the park. Look at where each type of rock is located. How can you tell which rocks are the oldest?

Waterfall Formation

More than 200,000 visitors hike to see the park's waterfalls every year. The waterfalls formed as rain fed streams and rivers in the Smokies. This moving water eroded some of the surrounding rock. Erosion created steep cliffs. Water cascaded down these cliffs and formed waterfalls.

The tallest waterfall is Ramsey Cascades. Another popular waterfall is Rainbow Falls. Beams of sunlight shining through the mist often produce rainbows.

BIOLOGICAL HISTORY

A great diversity of plant and animal life exists in Great Smoky Mountains National Park. Elk graze on grass in Cataloochee Valley. Carolina Northern flying squirrels glide from one yellow birch tree to another. Black bears scour through bushes in search of berries. The Smokies' climate and mountainous landscape allow all of these plant and animal species to coexist.

Biologists estimate the park is home to approximately 1,500 black bears.

Slime Mold Research

Two University of Georgia researchers were studying slime mold samples from Great Smoky Mountains National Park in 2003 when they made an unexpected discovery. They found that slime molds contain proteins called Hirano bodies. These proteins build up in the brains of people with Alzheimer's. Alzheimer's is a disease that affects memory and other brain functions. Scientists began experimenting on these slime molds to better understand the protein. They hope that understanding it better will enable them to find the cause and cure of Alzheimer's.

Animals in the Smokies

Elevation variations in Great Smoky Mountains National Park provide ideal habitats for many animals. Animals that prefer warm climates thrive in the lowlands. Those that prefer cooler climates can be found on mountain slopes.

Great Smoky Mountains National Park is known as the salamander capital of the world. More than 30 species of salamanders live in the park. Salamanders prefer warm and damp climates. Many live at low elevations amidst rocks and trees. Red-cheeked salamanders are the exception. They can be found at elevations of up to 3,000 feet (914 m). These salamanders have bright red, orange, or yellow patches on their cheeks. They can only be found in Great Smoky Mountains National Park. They do not live anywhere else in the world.

Wildlife enthusiasts often come to see black bears. Black bears can be found at all elevations in the park. They roam through its forests and along its mountain slopes.

Great Smoky Mountains National Park is also home to 12 species of bats. Bats may not be the most popular animals in the park. But they play an important role in maintaining the park's ecosystem. They help with pest control by eating mosquitoes. Some bats eat nectar in flowers. They pass pollen from one flower to another. This allows more flowers to grow.

A disease called white-nose syndrome is threatening many of the bats. This disease comes from a fungus that grows in caves. Bats live in caves. The fungus then infects bats. White-nose syndrome killed approximately 6 million bats in North America between 2006 and 2012. One of the species most affected by this disease is the little brown bat. Scientists believe this species may become extinct within 20 years. Research is being done to find out how to stop this disease from spreading.

One bat can eat as many as 3,000 insects each night.

Plants in the Smokies

More than 2,000 plant species flourish in Great Smoky Mountains National Park. Wildflowers bloom in the spring, when the Smokies receive a lot of rain. These include lady's slipper orchids and bleeding hearts. Lady's slipper orchids are delicate yellow or pink flowers with inflated pouches that look similar

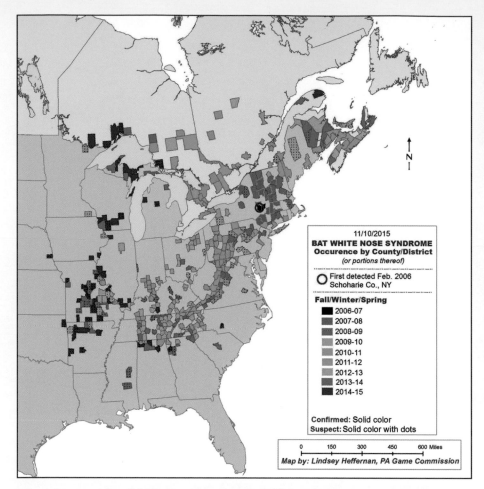

The Spread of White-Nose Syndrome

White-nose syndrome was first discovered in the United States in 2007. This map shows how the disease has spread since then. How can you tell from this map that the disease has affected many bats in Great Smoky Mountains National Park?

to slippers. Bleeding heart flowers have four pink heart-shaped petals.

Other plants thrive in the summer humidity. These include flowering shrubs such as the Catawba rhododendron. The Catawba rhododendron grows only at elevations greater than 3,500 feet (1,067 m). Its pink or purple flowers bloom in June. These shrubs often grow thick on mountain slopes.

FURTHER EVIDENCE

Chapter Three introduced you to the plants and animals that live in Great Smoky Mountains National Park. What was one of the main points of this chapter? What evidence is included to support this point? Read the article at the following website. Does the information on the website support the main point of the chapter? Does it present new evidence?

Wildlife in Great Smoky Mountains National Park

mycorelibrary.com/great-smoky-mountains

CHAPTER FOUR

HUMAN SETTLEMENT IN THE SMOKIES

Human settlement in the Smokies began thousands of years ago. Archaeologists have found tools in the area that are between 9,000 and 11,000 years old. These belonged to the Paleo-Indians. They may be the ancestors of some of the Cherokee Indians who live near the Smokies today.

Early Indians settled along rivers at the foothills of the mountains.

Approximately 11,000 members of the Eastern Band of Cherokees now live near Great Smoky Mountains National Park. They can trace back their history in this area more than 1,000 years. Their Cherokee ancestors built villages and lived off the land. They created a large network of trails. These trails allowed them to travel and trade goods between communities.

English-Cherokee Conflicts

The English had colonized South Carolina by the early 1700s. They encountered Cherokee Indians living in South Carolina and East Tennessee. They began to trade with the Cherokees. They traded European weapons for deer hides. This trading system benefited both the colonists and the Cherokees. But it was not long before conflict arose.

Cherokee Indians in the Smokies began suffering from foreign diseases such as smallpox. English colonists carried smallpox. The Cherokee had never encountered this disease before. It had devastating

The Cherokee felt threatened and wanted to protect their land and homes from the colonists.

effects on their population. The worst smallpox epidemic occurred in 1738. It killed approximately half of the tribe's members.

By the mid-1700s, English colonists had moved farther west. Their settlements edged closer to Cherokee lands. The Cherokee felt threatened. Tension between the two groups escalated. Some Cherokees captured horses that belonged to English colonists. The colonists then invaded Cherokee

Bent Trees

The trunks of many trees along trails in Great Smoky Mountains National Park are bent. Some people believe Cherokee Indians tied down these trees when they were saplings so they would grow to be bent. The Mountain Stewards organization believes these trees served as helpful markings for the Cherokee Indians. They may have pointed hunters toward water sources or toward caves where they could hide. Others, including some Cherokee elders, are not so sure this is the case. They think small earthquakes might have bent the trees.

territory. War between the colonists and the Cherokee continued for many years.

After the outbreak of the Revolutionary War (1775–1783), the Cherokee sided with the British. The British fought against the colonists. The colonists wanted independence from British rule. The Cherokee hoped the colonists would be defeated so they could reclaim some of their lost lands.

Cherokee Heritage

The British lost the Revolutionary War. Colonists then launched increasingly aggressive attacks on the Cherokee. They forced the Cherokee to sign treaties. These treaties gave the colonists more Cherokee lands. The Cherokee signed a final treaty in 1819. The colonists had taken the last of the Cherokee lands in the Smokies.

Cherokee Indians still lived in parts of the eastern United States. But President Andrew Jackson signed the Indian Removal Act in 1830. This act ordered American Indians living

Hiding in the Smokies

Some men who had signed up to fight in the American Civil War (1861–1865) later changed their minds. Some no longer believed in the war's cause. Many were simply tired of fighting. Some soldiers who deserted the army fled into the Smokies. The high elevation and rugged terrain protected them against potential enemies. They hid in caverns. They often repaired shoes for locals in exchange for food.

Museums on the reservation teach visitors about the Cherokee people's connection to the Smokies.

in the eastern United States to relocate west. A small group of Cherokees in western North Carolina avoided relocation. Businessman William H. Thomas successfully fought for their right to remain on their homeland. Thomas was a white man who had been adopted by a Cherokee leader.

Some of the Cherokees Thomas helped protect in the mid-1800s continued to live in the area into the early 1900s. They then lived peacefully alongside white settlers. The Cherokee Indian Reservation today is in North Carolina, on the south side of the park. Many Cherokee continue to pass on traditional craft skills to younger generations. The Cherokee have also allowed their reservation to be open to the public.

Russell Townsend is the Tribal Historic Preservation Officer for the Eastern Band of Cherokee Indians. He describes what Smoky Mountain life was like for Cherokee Indians before the park was created:

> *Prior to the park, the Eastern Band was a thriving community. . . . There was a lot of trade interaction; every community around here had something invested in the Eastern Band. They had to come get their corn ground here and come get their horses shoed here. They had to interact with Cherokee people on a regular basis. Prior to the federalization of lands in the early 1900s, there weren't really lines drawn, people didn't say that's a white community and this is a Cherokee community. They just said these are the people who live in this part of the mountains and we are all working together to make a living.*
>
> *Source: Mattea V. Sanders. "Giving Back Their Voice: The Eastern Band of Indians in the Twentieth Century." Native American Symposium. Southeastern Oklahoma State University, n.d. Web. Accessed April 22, 2016.*

What's the Big Idea?

Take a close look at this passage. How does Townsend describe Cherokee life before the creation of the park? How did the Cherokee and the white settlers interact in the early 1900s? How might their interactions have differed in the 1800s or earlier?

GREAT SMOKY MOUNTAINS NATIONAL PARK TODAY

Great Smoky Mountains National Park is the most-visited US national park for many reasons. Tourists are enchanted by its blue fog and forested peaks. Hikers come from all across the country to explore its many trails.

Hiking Trails

Great Smoky Mountains National Park has 850 miles (1,368 km) of hiking trails. They wind through the

The mild climate in Great Smoky Mountains National Park draws visitors all year long.

The Mountain Life Festival

Fall visitors to Great Smoky Mountains National Park can check out the Mountain Life Festival. This festival takes place at the Mountain Farm Museum. It celebrates the area's rich history. Volunteers demonstrate skills such as crafting chairs and making soap. Musicians play traditional folk music. These activities allow visitors to see what daily life was like for settlers in the 1800s and early 1900s.

Smokies at varied elevations. All of the trails offer hikers breathtaking views of the mountainous landscape.

One of the most popular trails is the Chimney Tops Trail. This trail winds alongside Sugarland Mountain on the north side of the park. It is only two miles (3.2 km) long. But it is a steep climb. It ascends 1,400 feet (427 m). High mountaintops that look similar to chimneys surround the trail. It crosses streams and meanders through thick forests.

The Appalachian Trail is one of the longest hiking trails in the United States. It stretches 2,190 miles

Visitors hike a trail on Mount Le Conte in the Smokies.

(3,524 km). It follows the Appalachian Mountains
through 14 US states. Part of the trail crosses through
Great Smoky Mountains National Park. It extends
more than 71 miles (114 km) from the east side of
the park to the west side. This segment of the hike
takes experienced hikers approximately seven days.
But most visitors prefer to hike shorter sections of
the trail. One of the most popular sections is the hike
to Charlies Bunion. Charlies Bunion is a large rock

outcropping in the center of the park. It juts out at an elevation of more than 6,000 feet (1,830 m). Hikers can view many distant mountains and valleys from this height.

Historic Buildings

Visitors can also explore the park's past by visiting historic structures. More than 90 historic buildings can be found throughout the park. These buildings allow visitors to see what life might have been like for early settlers in the 1800s and 1900s.

Charlies Bunion provides beautiful views of the surrounding Smokies.

Cades Cove on the west side of the park has a rich history of human settlement. The first Europeans began settling this valley in the 1820s. The population in the area grew to 271 people by 1830. They used timber to build wooden houses. They also built churches, barns, and a grain mill. All of these structures are preserved in Cades Cove now. Visitors

Park rangers in the Mountain Farm Museum explain what life was like for settlers.

can learn more about the history of these buildings through self-guided tours.

More historic buildings can be found at the Mountain Farm Museum. This museum is located on the south side near Oconaluftee Visitor Center. The National Park Service (NPS) moved historic buildings from throughout the Smokies to this site. These include a log house, a barn, and a working blacksmith shop. Smokies settlers built these structures in the late 1800s and early 1900s.

Historic buildings allow visitors to learn the human history of the park. Outdoor activities such as hiking allow them to explore its natural beauty. Both of these experiences allow visitors to appreciate all the park has to offer.

EXPLORE ONLINE

Chapter Five discusses popular activities and sights in Great Smoky Mountains National Park. The article at the website below goes into more depth on this topic. How is the information from the website the same as the information in Chapter Five? What new information did you learn from the website?

Things to Do in Great Smoky Mountains National Park

mycorelibrary.com/great-smoky-mountains

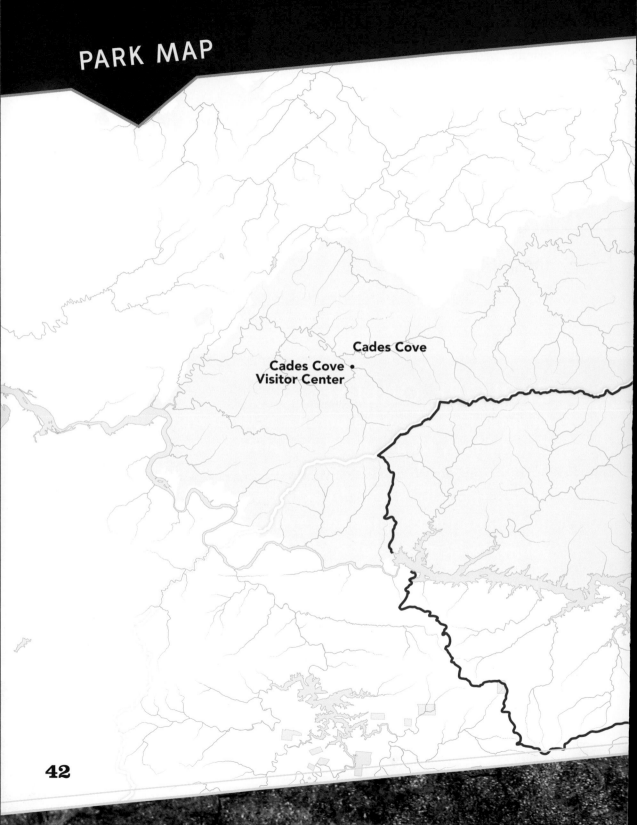

Cades Cove

Cades Cove •
Visitor Center

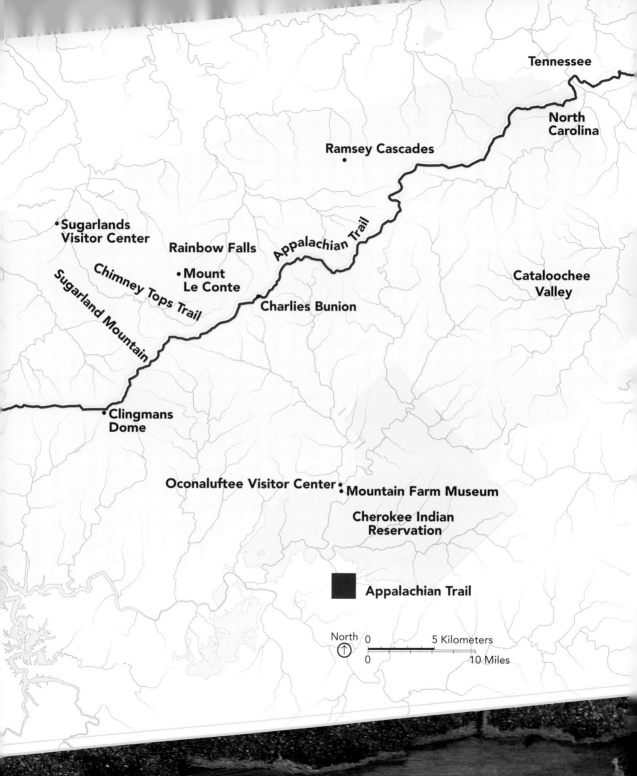

Tennessee

North Carolina

Ramsey Cascades

Appalachian Trail

Sugarlands Visitor Center

Rainbow Falls

Chimney Tops Trail

Mount Le Conte

Charlies Bunion

Cataloochee Valley

Sugarland Mountain

Clingmans Dome

Oconaluftee Visitor Center

Mountain Farm Museum

Cherokee Indian Reservation

Appalachian Trail

North

0   5 Kilometers

0   10 Miles

STOP AND THINK

Surprise Me

Chapter Four covers the history of human settlement in the Smokies. After reading this book, what two or three facts about the human history of Great Smoky Mountains National Park did you find most surprising? Write a few sentences about each fact. Why did you find each fact surprising?

Another View

This book discusses how Cherokee history is preserved in Great Smoky Mountains National Park. As you know, every source is different. Ask a librarian or another adult to help you find another source about this subject. Write a short essay comparing and contrasting the new source's point of view with that of this book's author. What is the point of view of each author? How are they similar and why? How are they different and why?

Tell the Tale

Chapter Five of this book describes some of the hiking paths visitors can explore in Great Smoky Mountains National Park. Imagine you are hiking along one of these paths. Write 200 words about your experience. What scenery do you notice?

You Are There

This book talks about early settlements in the Smokies. Imagine you are among the first people to settle there. Write a letter home telling your friends what you have found. What do you notice about the landscape? What plants and animals can you find? Be sure to add plenty of details to your notes.

GLOSSARY

archaeologist
a person who studies the bones and tools of ancient people to learn about the past

colonize
to take control of an area and send people to live there

ecosystem
a community of animals and plants living together

erode
to wear away

extinct
no longer existing

foreign
having to do with another country

fungus
a plant-like organism that has no leaves, flowers, or roots

habitat
the place and natural conditions in which a plant or an animal lives

lease
a document that allows someone to use land or property for a certain period of time

reservation
an area of land set aside by the government for a specific purpose

settler
someone who has made a home in a new place

syndrome
a disease that involves a particular group of symptoms

territory
a large area of land

LEARN MORE

Books

Maynard, Charles W. *Going to Great Smoky Mountains National Park.* Helena, MT: Farcountry, 2008.

National Parks Guide USA. Washington, DC: National Geographic Society, 2012.

Ogintz, Eileen. *The Kid's Guide to the Great Smoky Mountains.* Guilford, CT: Globe Pequot, 2016.

Websites

To learn more about National Parks, visit **booklinks.abdopublishing.com**. These links are routinely monitored and updated to provide the most current information available.

Visit **mycorelibrary.com** for free additional tools for teachers and students.

INDEX

ABOUT THE AUTHOR

Maddie Spalding is a writer from Minnesota. She enjoys writing about history and the environment. She has visited a few US national parks and hopes to visit more in the future.